Introduction

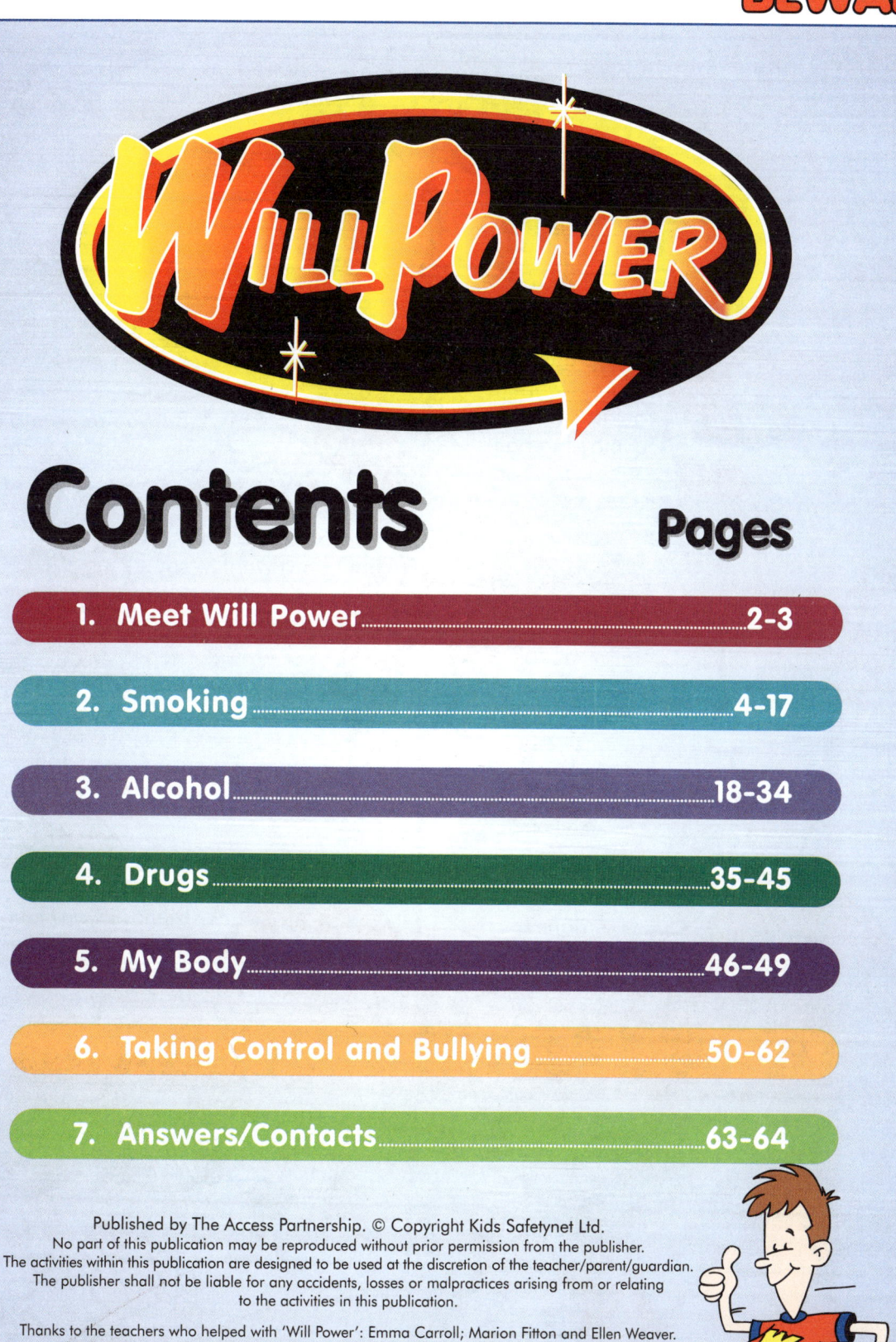

WillPower

Contents — Pages

1. Meet Will Power 2-3
2. Smoking 4-17
3. Alcohol 18-34
4. Drugs 35-45
5. My Body 46-49
6. Taking Control and Bullying 50-62
7. Answers/Contacts 63-64

Published by The Access Partnership. © Copyright Kids Safetynet Ltd.
No part of this publication may be reproduced without prior permission from the publisher.
The activities within this publication are designed to be used at the discretion of the teacher/parent/guardian.
The publisher shall not be liable for any accidents, losses or malpractices arising from or relating to the activities in this publication.

Thanks to the teachers who helped with 'Will Power': Emma Carroll; Marion Fitton and Ellen Weaver.
Thanks to Moston Lane Junior School and Arlies County Primary School for all their help.
Design: Jane Hart; Illustrations: Adrian Richardson.

1 Meet Will Power

BEWARE

School had just finished for the day...

"Stop dawdling Tim, I want to get to the park to play football!"

"I don't think I'll bother today Will. I'm not in the mood."

"But you're always in the mood for football."

"Well I'm not OK, just leave it."

"What's got into you? Is it something I've done?"

"No - it's not you, but I don't want to say, you might laugh."

"But I'm your best friend. I won't laugh."

It happened yesterday when I was at the park... You know Chris Tucker and that lot who hang around the bench.

Well they called me over...

"COME HERE TIM!"

2 Meet Will Power

1 Meet Will Power

They were laughing and being even louder than usual. Then I saw they were drinking cider and smoking.

What did you do?

I got scared and ran.

TRY SOME TIM.

COME BACK CHICKEN!

WHAT'S YOUR PROBLEM?

So you're worried that they'll be back again tonight?

Well yeah... sort of... I don't know...

What?... are you thinking of trying them?

Well... maybe... I can't decide. You see I don't know much about them.

Will came up with a suggestion...

Well instead of going to the park, why don't we find out as much as we can about how alcohol and tobacco can affect us.

Good idea Will, then I can make a choice knowing the facts.

Come on then, let's get started...

2 Smoking

The History of Tobacco

Tobacco comes from a large plant that can grow up to 3m high. Its large leaves are hung up to dry before being turned into smoking tobacco.

In the old days, some doctors thought of tobacco as a kind of medicine and gave it to their patients to smoke. Nowadays doctors know differently and that smoking is bad for you.

Tobacco was first introduced to this country in the 16th century, by a man called Sir Walter Raleigh who with other explorers, found tobacco growing in the New World (what we call America today).

In those days, tobacco was always smoked through a pipe.

However, even then, there were people who were against smoking, in fact King James I tried to ban it until they realised that if they taxed tobacco, they could make a lot of money from it.

Snuff is another kind of tobacco which was very fashionable in the eighteenth century. It was powdered and people used to put some on their hand and sniff it up their nose!

Cigarettes were not used until the 19th century when during the Crimean War, British soldiers learned to roll tobacco in paper. By the end of the century, machines had been invented to mass-produce cigarettes and cigarette factories were opening in Britain.

At first, smoking was something that only men did but gradually women began to smoke too.

No one seemed to realise the dangers of the habit until 1962 when the Royal College of Physicians published its first report on the subject of smoking and health.

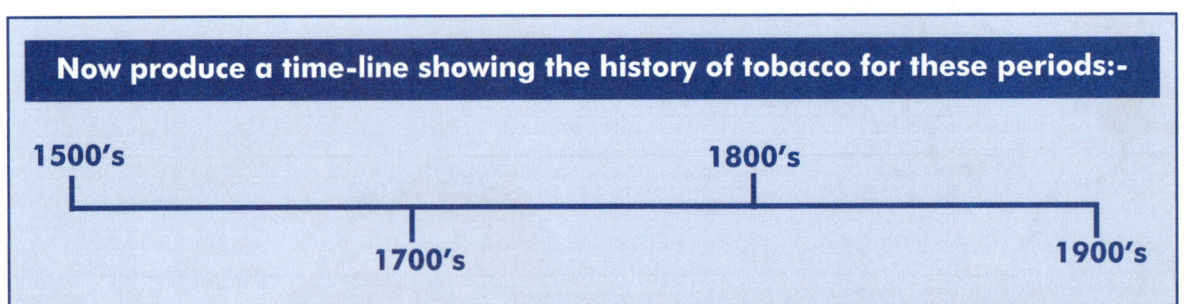

Now produce a time-line showing the history of tobacco for these periods:-

1500's   1800's
      1700's   1900's

2 Smoking

Some Facts about Smoking

- In Great Britain approximately 450 children start smoking every day.
- It is illegal to sell any tobacco product to anyone below the age of 16.
- Tobacco contains over 4000 chemicals in the form of particles and gases.

- More than 17,000 children under the age of five are admitted to hospital every year because of the effects of passive smoking. They breathe in smoke in homes and public places where people smoke.
- Some of the immediate effects of passive smoking include eye irritation, headache, cough, sore throat, dizziness and nausea.

- Each year 120,000 people in the UK die from smoking related diseases, accounting for one fifth of all deaths.
- Passive smoking contributes to 600 lung cancer deaths a year and up to 12,000 cases of heart diseases in non smokers.
- Smoking related illnesses account for 8 million visits to the doctors and over 7 million prescriptions each year.

Smoking 5

2 Smoking

True or False

Recently a friend of Will Power offered him a cigarette. Will refused, he had seen a video about smoking and knew how dangerous it can be. Will felt that knowing the facts about smoking helped him make the decision not to smoke.

**Do you know any facts about smoking?
Put a ring round either true or false for each statement below.**

Smoking can cause cancer.

TRUE

FALSE

Smoking can make you cough.

TRUE

FALSE

Smoking is bad for your health.

TRUE

FALSE

Cigarettes are made from tobacco.

TRUE

FALSE

You can become addicted to cigarettes.

TRUE

FALSE

You can tell if someone has just had a cigarette because of the way they smell.

TRUE   FALSE

2 Smoking

What are Cigarettes?

There is no one reason why people smoke but many people say it helps them to cope with stress when they are at work, even though they know it is bad for their health.

DO YOU KNOW ANYONE THAT SMOKES?
If you do, ask them why they do it.

People smoke cigars and pipes, but the most common thing to smoke is a cigarette. Cigarettes are made from tobacco, which comes from the leaf of a plant.

When you light a cigarette, the tobacco burns and gives off a lot of chemicals and gases which you breathe into your lungs:

NICOTINE — This is the drug in tobacco that people think helps them to relax. They are wrong! Nicotine actually makes your heart beat faster.

CARBON MONOXIDE — This gas can leave you out of breath when you inhale it.

TAR — When you breathe in cigarette smoke, a horrible, smelly, sticky thing called tar is left in your lungs. The more you smoke, the more tar you get in your lungs. This can lead to serious diseases.

SMOKING CAN ALSO HARM OTHER PARTS OF YOUR BODY TOO

80% of heart attacks are smoking related

95% of people who have bronchitis are smokers.

Can you draw a poster showing all the harmful chemicals found in tobacco?

Smoking 7

2 Smoking

You and Smoking

Have you ever tried a cigarette?
Believe it or not, some children are as young as five when they smoke their first cigarette. Most young people who smoke actually admit they don't really like it and only do it because it makes them feel like grown ups. **Don't you think that is silly?**
Other people say they don't want to say **'no'** if someone offers them a cigarette because it makes them look **'soft'**.

Do you know what the law is about cigarettes?

- It is against the law to sell cigarettes to children under 16 - even if they are buying them for someone else.

- All cigarette packets must have a Government Health Warning on them. These warn you that tobacco can seriously damage your health.

- Tobacco companies are not allowed to advertise on TV but they can sponsor sporting events.

Do you think it makes sense that tobacco companies can be linked to sporting events? Give a reason for your answer.

_____
_____
_____
_____
_____

2 Smoking

Smoking Quiz (ALL CLUES ACROSS)

1. Smoking damages your _____ (5)
2. The drug in tobacco is called _____ (8)
3. Smokers' lungs become filled with sticky _____ (3)
4. Cigarettes make your _____ smell. (6)
5. Breathing in a smoky atmosphere is called _____ smoking. (7)
6. Packets of cigarettes must carry a Government _____ warning. (6)
7. Cigarettes are made from _____ (7)
8. Carbon monoxide stops _____ getting to parts of your body. (6)

Smoking 9

2 Smoking

Other side effects of smoking...

Will has found out that smoking not only damages your health, it also has other unpleasant side effects.

Passive Smoking...

Smoke from a cigarette can annoy other people. It can irritate their eyes and make them cough when they breathe in. It is called **PASSIVE SMOKING**.

Fire...

Smoking can also cause fire if cigarettes are not put out properly. Hundreds of people are killed each year from fires caused this way.

Cost...

A packet of 20 cigarettes can cost more than £4.00. Some people smoke more than one packet a day - *that's a lot of money!*

Smell...

Cigarette smoke can make your hair, breath, clothes and house smell horrible!

Stains...

Have you ever noticed that some people have yellow stains on their fingers and teeth? This is caused by the tar in cigarettes and is very difficult to scrub off.

2 Smoking

Other side effects of smoking...

Will would like your help. He wants to make people aware of the side effects of smoking. He thinks that if people know all the bad things about smoking they are less likely to start.

Can you create a poster letting people know some of the side effects of smoking? Use the information on the previous page to help you.

Smoking 11

2 Smoking

A Smoke-Free Society

The best way not to smoke is to never start. Do you know anybody who wants to give up smoking? If you do, tell them about what you have learned about smoking and what it does to their body.

Below is a plan for giving up smoking. Why not turn it into a poster and give it to the person who wants to give up.

1 Think hard about WHY you want to stop smoking.
Read as much as you can about the subject, and make a list of all the bad things smoking means to you.

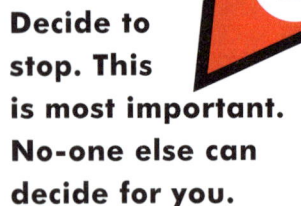

2 Decide to stop. This is most important. No-one else can decide for you.

NEVER AGAIN!

3 Prepare yourself for stopping.
Work out when and where you smoke.

12 Smoking

2 Smoking

4 List the ways you could change the habits and fight temptation.

5 Buy in lots of nibbles and non-fattening drinks. Make a plan.

6 Stop smoking. Set a date in the near future and stick to it. Make it a special day. Treat yourself.

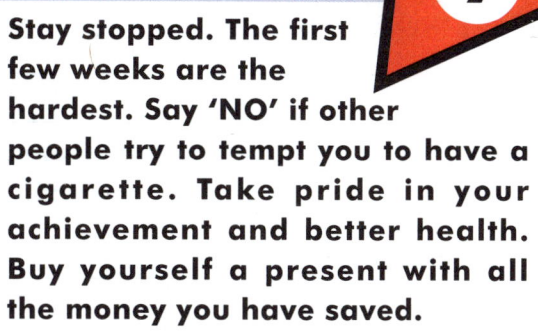

7 Stay stopped. The first few weeks are the hardest. Say 'NO' if other people try to tempt you to have a cigarette. Take pride in your achievement and better health. Buy yourself a present with all the money you have saved.

2 Smoking

Exploding some myths

Will has been asking people why they smoke. He has found out some of the most common reasons people give for smoking. He has come up with answers that 'explode these myths'.

■ **Smoking looks cool, sophisticated, tough and grown up.**

WRONG

It makes people smelly.
It stains people's teeth and fingers.

■ **Smoking calms your nerves**

WRONG

If it does, it does so at the expense of your health. Perhaps it keeps people calm while they worry about how much money they are spending or why they cough so much.

2 Smoking

BEWARE

■ Smoking helps keep your weight down

WRONG

Some people eat more for a little while after giving up smoking because food tastes so much nicer. It doesn't take long to get back to normal though.

■ Smoking gives you confidence

WRONG

Most confident people are confident because of themselves, not because they are holding a cigarette.

Everyone is good at something and has their own worth. Nobody needs dried tobacco leaves wrapped in paper to prove themselves.

Smoking 15

2 Smoking

Some Effects of Smoking

Look at the picture below and write down some of the effects of smoking in the spaces provided.

2 Smoking

Individual Views

JULIE (aged 18)

"I didn't mean to get started, I just used to smoke at the disco because everyone else seemed to. Then when I started work, I found I was doing it all the time. Now I wish I could stop. I half wish they'd ban it at work, that might help. I know it's such a waste of money and I know it's not doing me any good but I still carry on. Stupid isn't it? I wish I'd never had that first cigarette."

Why does Julie wish she had never started smoking?
_____
_____

MARK (aged 15)

"My friends used to offer me cigarettes. They acted like it was cool. I tried it a few times. Then when we did a project at school and I learned a few of the facts about smoking I just thought never again. It's not for me. I love playing sports and smoking mucks that up. And I don't want to catch a horrible disease."

Why has Mark decided not to start smoking?
_____
_____
_____

Smoking 17

3 Alcohol

Alcoholic and Non-alcoholic

Will Power and his mother were getting ready for a party they were having at their house. Will had to help his mum get the drinks ready. She asked Will to sort them into alcoholic and non-alcoholic groups. **Can you help him?**

Lager | Alco Pop | Coke | Bitter | Wine | Orange Juice | Whisky | Lemonade

ALCOHOLIC	NON-ALCOHOLIC

Will asked his mum why adults could drink alcohol and children couldn't. She explained that because children's bodies were smaller, the poison in alcohol could affect them more than it would in an adults' bigger body.

Will realised he didn't know much about alcohol, so he decided to find out more…

3 Alcohol

What is Alcohol?

Alcohol is brewed or distilled from cereals, grapes, fruit or even vegetables. It is often flavoured with herbs to give it a distinctive taste. Alcohol, is a poison which can harm your body if you drink too much.

Beer is made from hops, grains and yeast. Grapes are used to make wine. Spirits are made of grains which have been boiled and then cooled. Alcohol has different effects on different people. The more you drink the greater the effect.

Like smoking, people say that alcohol helps to relieve stress and makes them happier. This may be true in small amounts but drinking a lot of alcohol can be very dangerous.

Alcohol is a chemical. It is made by tiny living things called yeast. There are many sorts of yeast, only some of which can be drunk. Yeast can be found on fruit skins and any sugary substance will turn into alcohol if it is left long enough. The alcohol that people drink comes in three main forms - beer, wines and spirits.

There are other forms of alcohol which **ARE NOT DRINKABLE**. Alcohol is found in shoe polish, window cleaning creams and de-icing sprays for car windows.

What is alcohol?
_____

The alcohol people drink comes in three main forms. What are they?
1. _____ 2. _____ 3. _____

Beer is made from _____

Spirits are made from _____

Alcohol 19

3 Alcohol

What is Alcohol?

ALCOHOL IS A DRUG.
In small amounts it can produce a feeling of well-being but in larger amounts it affects the drinker's ability to do things, their judgement and even their behaviour.

Alcohol has a number of damaging effects. It kills brain cells and irritates the lining of the stomach. If someone drinks a lot over a long period of time, it can cause liver disease and makes heart disease more likely.

Drinking alcohol and driving is extremely dangerous. Even a small amount of alcohol can slow down your reactions. Never let anyone drive if they have been drinking alcohol, it is extremely dangerous.

Most people drink in sensible amounts, however, alcohol can be addictive. In the UK and around the world there are many people whose drinking habits have caused themselves their friends and families serious harm.

A PERSON WHO NEEDS ALCOHOL CONSTANTLY IS KNOWN AS AN ALCOHOLIC

THE LAW SAYS THAT:

- When you are 14 you can go into a bar if you are with an adult. You cannot buy anything.

- When you are 16 you may drink some kinds of alcohol, but only if you are eating a meal.

- At 18 you may buy alcohol on your own.

3 Alcohol

BEWARE

Different Drinks

In the space below, list all the types of drinks that you can think of. Think about what drinks you have at home, what drinks your parents have and what drinks you have seen on TV.

_____
_____
_____
_____
_____
_____
_____

Now list all these drinks under the different headings below:

HOT	COLD	DRINKS FOR CHILDREN	DRINKS FOR ADULTS

What is your favourite drink?

_____
_____

Alcohol 21

3 Alcohol

Strength of Alcohol

Different drinks have different strengths, which is why they come in different sized bottles or are served in different sized glasses.

> *Doctors tell adults they could damage their health if they consume more alcohol than the following guidelines:-*
>
> A LIMIT FOR MEN IS 21 UNITS / WOMEN IS 14 UNITS A WEEK

It takes the liver an hour to process one unit of alcohol. Binge drinking is where a lot of units are drunk in a short period of time. This can be extremely dangerous and could cause the body harm.

Small glass of wine — 1 unit	Large glass of wine — 2 units
Half pint of normal lager — 1 unit	1 pint of normal lager — 2 units
Half pint of strong lager — 2 units	1 pint of strong lager — 4 units
Single whisky — 1 unit	1 small bottle of alcopops — 1 unit

Not all alcoholic drinks have the same amount of alcohol in them. That is why a small glass of whisky has the same number of units as a big glass of beer.

3 Alcohol

Why do people drink?

Will decided to find out why people drink. He interviewed people and these were the main reasons people gave.

What do you think of these reasons?

"Because all my friends drink - I don't want to be left out, do I?"

"It impresses people."

"It helps me to overcome my shyness."

"I really like the taste, honestly I do."

"I want to see how it feels to be drunk."

"There's nothing else to do"

Can you think of other things people could do instead of drinking?

_____
_____
_____
_____

Alcohol

3 Alcohol

Pub Signs

Look at the typical pub signs below.
Do you think there is a history behind the signs?

GEORGE & DRAGON

Explain: _____

THE KINGS HEAD

Explain: _____

THE BREWERS ARMS

Explain: _____

THE WHITE HART

Explain: _____

THE BEEHIVE

Explain: _____

THE QUEEN VICTORIA

Explain: _____

A lot of socialising in Britain is based around public houses (pubs). Can you think of three soap operas from TV where there is a pub which acts as a focal point? Discuss your answers in class.

3 Alcohol

In the space below, draw your own sign for a non-alcoholic bar

What are you going to call it?

What will you serve?

Alcohol 25

3 Alcohol

Some more facts about alcohol

1 Alcohol reaches the brain and slows down the activity within five minutes of being swallowed.

2 Alcopops might taste like a soft drink but they contain spirits and are extremely strong.

3 Alcohol affects women more quickly than it does men.

4 The lighter your body weight, the greater the effects of the alcohol.

5 Nearly 90% of boys in England have drunk alcohol by the time they are 13.

3 Alcohol

BEWARE

Alcoholic and Non-Alcoholic

Some drinks have alcohol in them, some drinks don't. Can you unscramble the names of drinks below and put them into lists of alcoholic and non-alcoholic drinks?

1. REGAL _____
2. IEML _____
3. IWEN _____
4. REDIC _____
5. YWSIKH _____
6. KIML _____
7. YBRADN _____
8. AET _____
9. ING _____
10. OALC _____
11. EREB _____
12. PCAHGANME _____

ALCOHOLIC DRINKS	NON-ALCOHOLIC DRINKS

Alcohol 27

3 Alcohol

Wordsearch

Now you have unscrambled the words on the previous page, can you find them in the wordsearch below?

L	W	T	E	A	E	B	R	H	J
A	R	G	H	J	H	N	M	Q	E
G	C	O	L	A	G	N	I	O	P
E	O	I	A	E	B	R	T	W	Y
R	Z	U	X	B	N	E	G	I	N
A	Q	S	S	L	L	H	G	N	I
S	W	W	M	I	L	K	Q	E	V
Y	H	U	I	M	O	P	L	K	F
C	I	B	E	E	T	Y	U	U	B
I	S	S	E	A	C	C	V	R	R
D	K	Y	U	E	P	X	P	P	A
E	Y	C	F	G	R	L	T	R	N
R	O	I	U	T	G	A	H	H	D
A	R	E	V	E	Y	I	M	C	Y
C	H	A	M	P	A	G	N	E	C

1. _ _ _ _ _ _
2. _ _ _ _
3. _ _ _ _
4. _ _ _ _ _
5. _ _ _ _ _ _
6. _ _ _ _
7. _ _ _ _ _ _
8. _ _ _
9. _ _ _
10. _ _ _ _
11. _ _ _ _
12. _ _ _ _ _ _ _ _ _

28 Alcohol

3 Alcohol

Drinking Questionnaire

Find out who drinks what in your family by asking them to fill in a questionnaire. Here are some suggestions for questions you may wish to ask:

1. How often do you drink alcohol?
   _____

2. What do you drink?
   _____

3. Do you have a favourite brand?
   _____

4. Where do you drink? (Pub, at home, restaurant etc.)
   _____

5. Why do you drink?
   _____

6. When did you start drinking?
   _____

7. Do you know anyone who has a drink problem?
   _____

8. How much do you drink a week?
   _____

9. Do you know the maximum alcohol limit for a man and a woman each week as recommended by doctors?
   _____

3 Alcohol

A visit to a Country Pub

Will Power has been to the seaside with his family and his best friend Tim. On the way home Grandad Parkin suggests they all stop off for a drink at a country pub.

PRICE LIST

BEER	1 pint	2 units	£2.20
LOW ALCOHOL BEER	bottle	1/3 unit	£1.10
CIDER	1/2 pint	1 1/2 units	£1.15
WINE	glass	1 unit	£2.00
GIN	pub measure	1 unit	£1.50
WHISKY	pub measure	1 unit	£1.50
COLA	bottle	0 units	£1.00
TONIC	small bottle	0 units	£1.00
FRUIT JUICE	small bottle	0 units	£1.00
CRISPS	1 packet	0 units	£0.50

3 Alcohol

A visit to a Country Pub

Using the price list on the previous page, can you fill in the cost of the drinks and the units of alcohol?

MUM	COST	UNITS
1 Cola		
2 Fruit Juices		
Crisps		
TOTAL		

GRANDAD PARKIN	COST	UNITS
Bottle of Low Alcohol Beer		
Crisps		
Cola		
TOTAL		

NANA MEL	COST	UNITS
3 Gins		
2 Tonics		
TOTAL		

KAREN	COST	UNITS
3 x		
½ Pint of Cider		
Crisps		
TOTAL		

TIM	COST	UNITS
3 Colas		
2 Crisps		
TOTAL		

WILL POWER	COST	UNITS
1 Cola		
1 Fruit Juice		
Crisps		
TOTAL		

Alcohol

3 Alcohol

BEWARE

A Visit to a Country Pub

Can you answer the questions about Will and his family's trip to the pub?

1 What is the total cost for the drinks and crisps?

2 Who had the most units of alcohol?

3 Why did Will and Tim only have non-alcoholic drinks?

4 Who do you think was driving home? Why?

5 If the family go out once a month and spend the same amount, how much would they spend in a year?

32 Alcohol

3 Alcohol

BEWARE

Non-Drinkers

When Will Power was talking to adults about drinking alcohol, he found out some of them didn't drink. He found out five of the main reasons. They are.....

Religion...

Religion is the main reason why many people don't drink alcohol.

Moslems, Quakers and members of the Salvation Army are just some.

Medical Reasons...

- Some people choose not to drink because of medical conditions such as heart or liver diseases.
- Pregnant women usually avoid alcohol.
- People taking certain medicines are also advised not to drink.

Work...

Sometimes a person's job may influence their choice. People who drive for a living and people who work machinery shouldn't drink whilst at work because they have to be in control at all times.

Don't Like it...

Some people have tried alcoholic drinks but haven't liked them. They might not like the taste or the way it affects them.

Alcohol Problem...

Some people have an alcohol problem. They have drunk too much in the past and must avoid it in case they become addicted again.

What do you think Will Power discovered about non-drinkers?

Alcohol 33

3 Alcohol

Alternative to Alcohol

Some people say they must drink alcohol to be happy. This may mean they are mis-using alcohol by drinking too much, too often. Others say they need to drink alcohol to get to sleep, but have they tried reading a book, a hot relaxing bath or even a cup of warm milk?

Can you design a poster giving people some alternatives to drinking alcohol as a way of making themselves happy?

34 Alcohol

4 Drugs

What are Drugs?

When Will Power was finding out about alcohol he came across a definition of a drug:

> **A DRUG IS: - ANY SUBSTANCE WHICH CAN AFFECT YOUR BODY OR YOUR MIND**

Will decided to find out if alcohol and tobacco were drugs. He has written down some of the effects of smoking cigarettes and drinking alcohol.

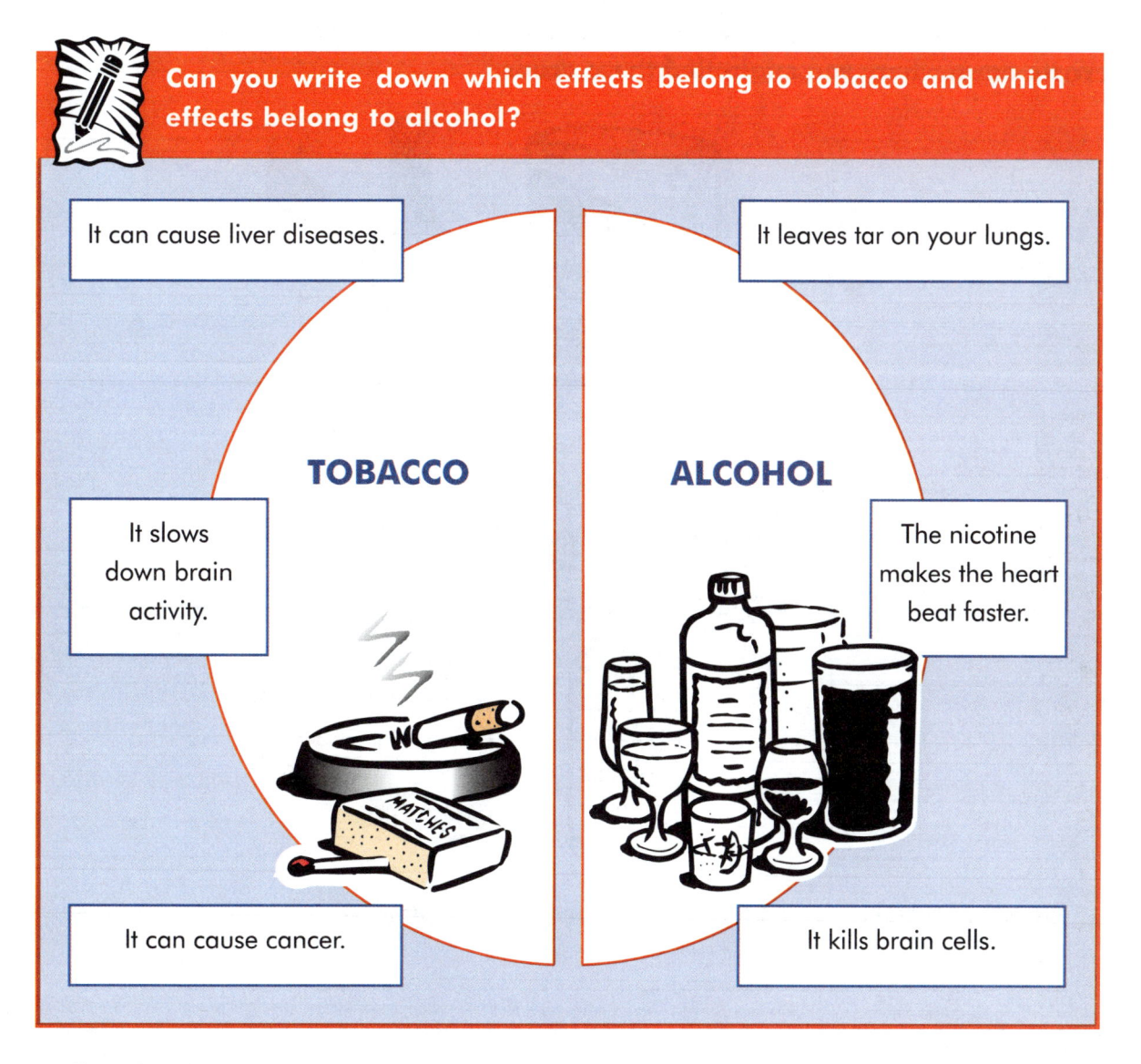

Can you write down which effects belong to tobacco and which effects belong to alcohol?

TOBACCO

- It can cause liver diseases.
- It slows down brain activity.
- It can cause cancer.

ALCOHOL

- It leaves tar on your lungs.
- The nicotine makes the heart beat faster.
- It kills brain cells.

Will realised that both tobacco and alcohol were drugs. He thought there might be more to drugs. He decided to find out...

4 Drugs

BEWARE

REMEMBER All medicines are drugs – but not all drugs are medicines

When you are ill, the doctor will often give you medicine to take, which will help to make you better. These kind of drugs are OK to take as long as you follow the instructions and as long as they have been given to you by a sensible person in a position of authority like a doctor, a parent or carer.

Often these drugs will be kept in a safe place in bottles with special lids so that little children cannot open them. But do you know where we can find drugs which aren't medicines?
Write down where you might find these drugs.

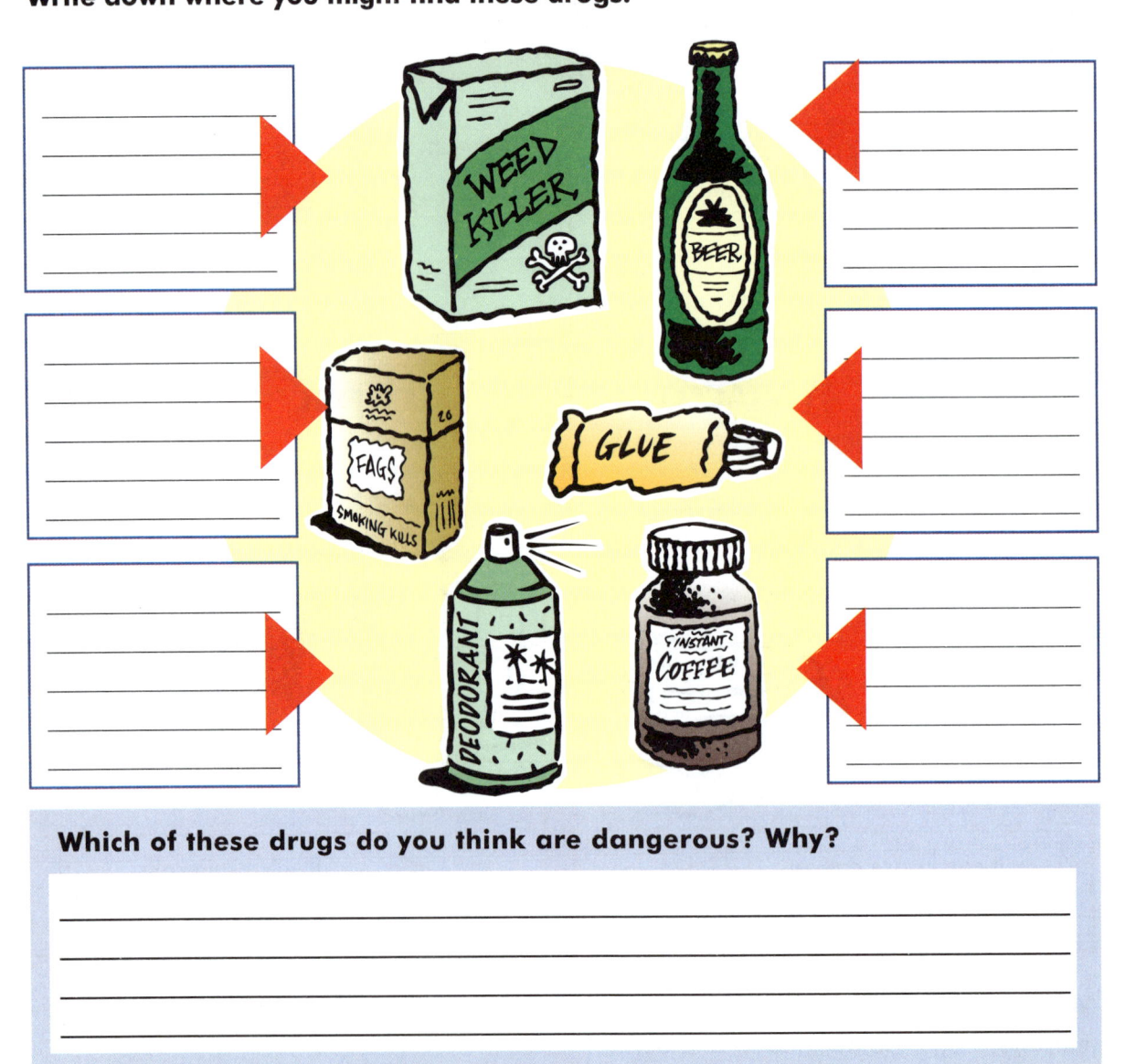

(Images: Weed Killer, Beer, Fags (Smoking Kills), Glue, Deodorant, Instant Coffee)

Which of these drugs do you think are dangerous? Why?

36 Drugs

4 Drugs

Dangerous Drugs

We know that some people use drugs which are not medicines, like tobacco and alcohol which can both become addictive if used frequently. Some people use other drugs as well, which are illegal. Have you heard of things like cannabis, cocaine and heroin?
Why do you think people use drugs like this?

_____
_____
_____

All drugs whether from a pub, shop, a doctor or an illegal dealer are potentially dangerous. People can become addicted to legal drugs like alcohol, prescription medicines like tranquillisers and sleeping pills as well as illegal drugs like cocaine and heroin.

In the space below, draw an anti-drugs poster warning people about the dangers of becoming addicted to drugs.

Drugs 37

4 Drugs

Making Decisions

As you grow up, you must make more and more decisions for yourself. You must decide what you want to do, which won't always be the same as your friends. Everybody is different. At the moment a lot of different people and things will be influencing the decisions you make.

Tick which of these things you think influence you?

- ☐ mum & dad
- ☐ brothers & sisters
- ☐ school teachers
- ☐ TV & radio
- ☐ newspapers
- ☐ friends
- ☐ myself
- ☐ anything else

Do you agree that some people are better at helping you to make up your mind than other people? **Who are they?**

_____
_____
_____
_____
_____
_____

Is there anyone who you think you shouldn't listen to? Who?

_____
_____
_____
_____
_____
_____
_____

4 Drugs

How much do you know about the effects of drugs?

For each numbered statement, put a ring round either True or False.

1 TRUE FALSE
- A drug is a substance that causes changes in the body or mind.

2 TRUE FALSE
- As a rule, women need less alcohol than men to get drunk.

3 TRUE FALSE
- Cigarette smokers only harm themselves.

4 TRUE FALSE
- A few drops of nicotine on the tongue can kill a healthy adult.

5 TRUE FALSE
- People can do things better after a few drinks.

6 TRUE FALSE
- Black coffee sobers you up if you have been drinking.

4 Drugs

ANSWERS

1 ☐ A drug is a substance that causes changes in the body or mind.

TRUE / FALSE

A drug is a substance that alters the way in which the body works. No matter how a drug is taken, it enters the blood and is carried to the brain. And we already know that the brain controls the rest of the body.

TRUE / FALSE

Women do get drunk on less alcohol because they usually weigh less than men and men have more water in their bodies than women so the alcohol is diluted more quickly.

2 ☐ As a rule, women need less alcohol than men to get drunk.

3 ☐ Cigarette smokers only harm themselves.

TRUE / **FALSE**

Inhaling tobacco smoke from other people's cigarettes can harm the lungs. This is called passive smoking and is the reason why smoking is banned in many public places.

40 Drugs

4 Drugs

ANSWERS

4

■ A few drops of nicotine on the tongue can kill a healthy adult.

(TRUE) FALSE

Pure nicotine is a highly poisonous substance. Very small amounts can cause severe illness.

TRUE (FALSE)

People may think they can do things better, but they can't!

5

■ People can do things better after a few drinks.

6

■ Black coffee sobers you up if you have been drinking.

TRUE (FALSE)

It may stop people feeling drowsy but it will not speed up the time it takes for your liver to process the alcohol.

Drugs 41

4 Drugs

What would you do in the following situations?

1 You are at scout camp with your friends. After lights out, Johnny, one of the older boys, asks you and a friend to come outside and have a cigarette. You don't want to say no because your friends will laugh at you, but you know smoking is bad for you. And you don't want to be caught by Mr Hedges the scoutmaster either. **WHAT DO YOU DO?**

_____
_____
_____

2 You are in the park playing with your friend Sonia. Sonia's elder sister is there too, with some of her friends from school. They have bought a bottle of cider and seem to be drunk. They offer you some. **WHAT DO YOU DO?**

_____
_____
_____
_____

42 Drugs

4 Drugs

BEWARE

3
You are walking home from school when you find a pound coin in the gutter. Your friend Siraz says that he knows a shop where they sell individual cigarettes to under age children. He hassles you to come with him and buy some. **WHAT DO YOU DO?**

4
One Saturday you go into the town centre to do some shopping. You see Robert, a boy from your class, hanging around with some rough kids. Robert is staggering and you see a tube of glue in his pocket. You are worried that Robert has been glue sniffing. **WHAT DO YOU DO?**

Can you draw a situation that you would find hard to deal with?
Get someone to help you come up with a way of dealing with it?

Drugs

4 Drugs

The History of Medicine

A man called Vesalius, who lived in the 1500s, was the first person to make detailed observations after dissecting human bodies. Many of the bodies were stolen from recently dug graves!

An English doctor, William Harvey, showed that the heart pumps blood round the body in one direction in a continuous loop. This was a very important discovery.

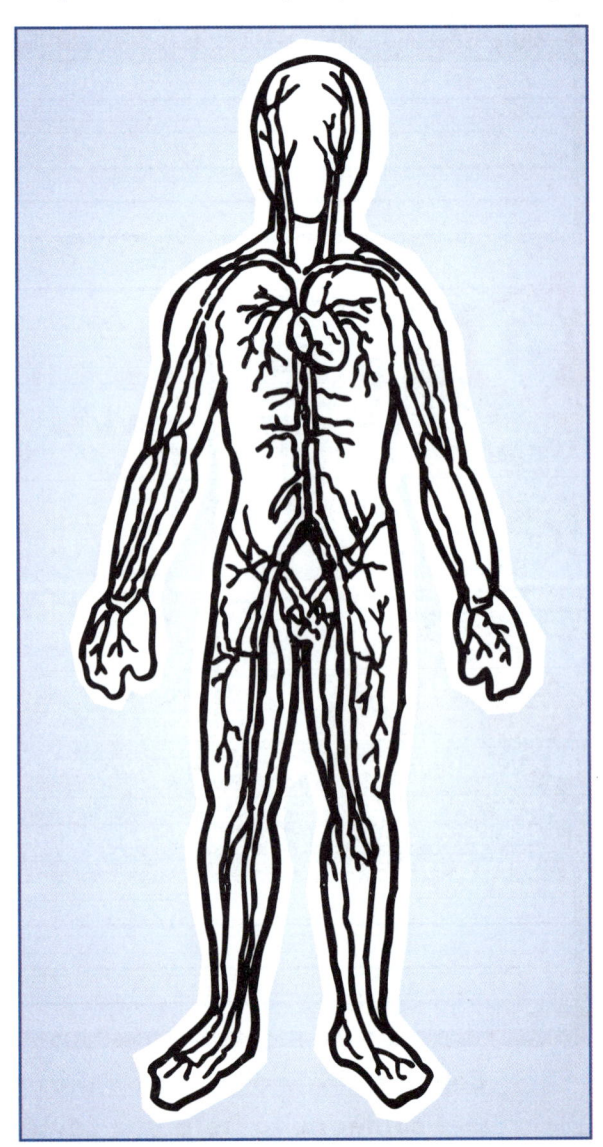

The first doctor was an ancient Egyptian called Imhotep, who lived in about 1650 BC.

The 'Father of Medicine' is a Greek called Hippocrates, who lived in the 4th Century BC. He knew the importance of hygiene and a good diet, and helped to develop medicine as a science, based on careful observation and record keeping.

Galen was the most famous doctor in the Roman world. He was a surgeon at a school for gladiators, where he learnt about the body's structure. He developed his knowledge by dissecting animals.

44 Will Power

4 Drugs

In 1796, a doctor called Edward Jenner introduced a new vaccination against Smallpox, a very deadly disease.

A few years later, laughing gas was discovered. It meant a patient could be kept conscious but not feel so much pain during an operation. A chemical called ether was later used as the first anaesthetic.

Florence Nightingale was a famous English woman who developed modern nursing. She led a team of nurses during the Crimean War in the 1850s, who cared for British soldiers and greatly improved conditions for the soldiers while they were in hospital.

A very important discovery was made by Louis Pasteur, a French professor of Chemistry, at the end of the nineteenth century. He demonstrated that germs enter wounds and cause disease, proving that germs did not simply grow out of the wound as doctors had thought previously.

He gave his name to pasteurisation, which is the process of rapidly heating and cooling a liquid to kill harmful bacteria. He first used the idea to stop his wine going off - today we use it to keep milk fresh.

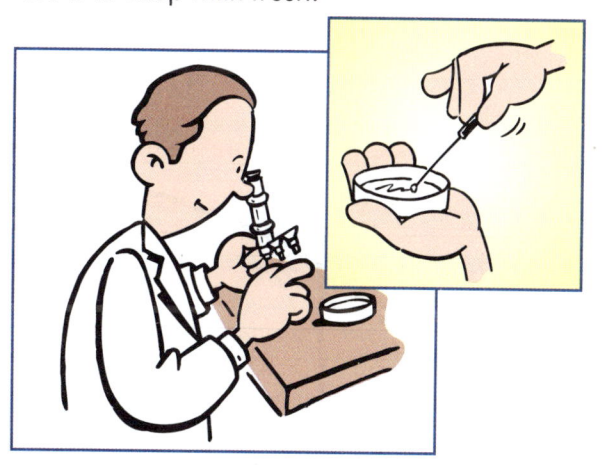

How did Hippocrates develop medicine as a science?
_____

What did William Harvey discover?
_____

Why did laughing gas help patients?
_____

Who was Florence Nightingale?
_____

What did Louis Pasteur discover?
_____

Will Power

5   My Body

Do you know how your body works?

Inside your body are lots of different working parts called organs, each doing an important job that helps to keep you alive.

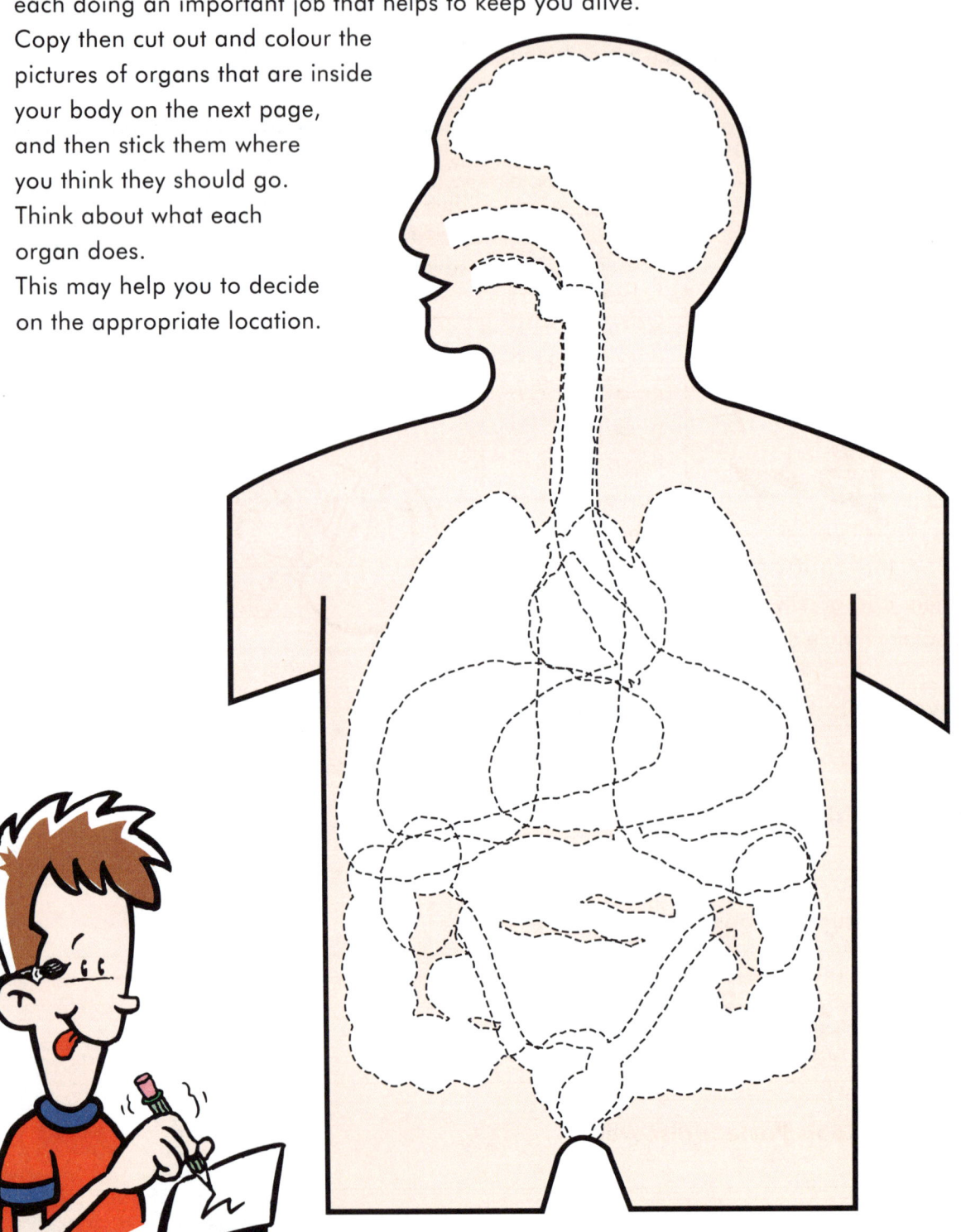

Copy then cut out and colour the pictures of organs that are inside your body on the next page, and then stick them where you think they should go. Think about what each organ does.

This may help you to decide on the appropriate location.

46   My Body

5 My Body

These organs can be copied then cut out and coloured in.

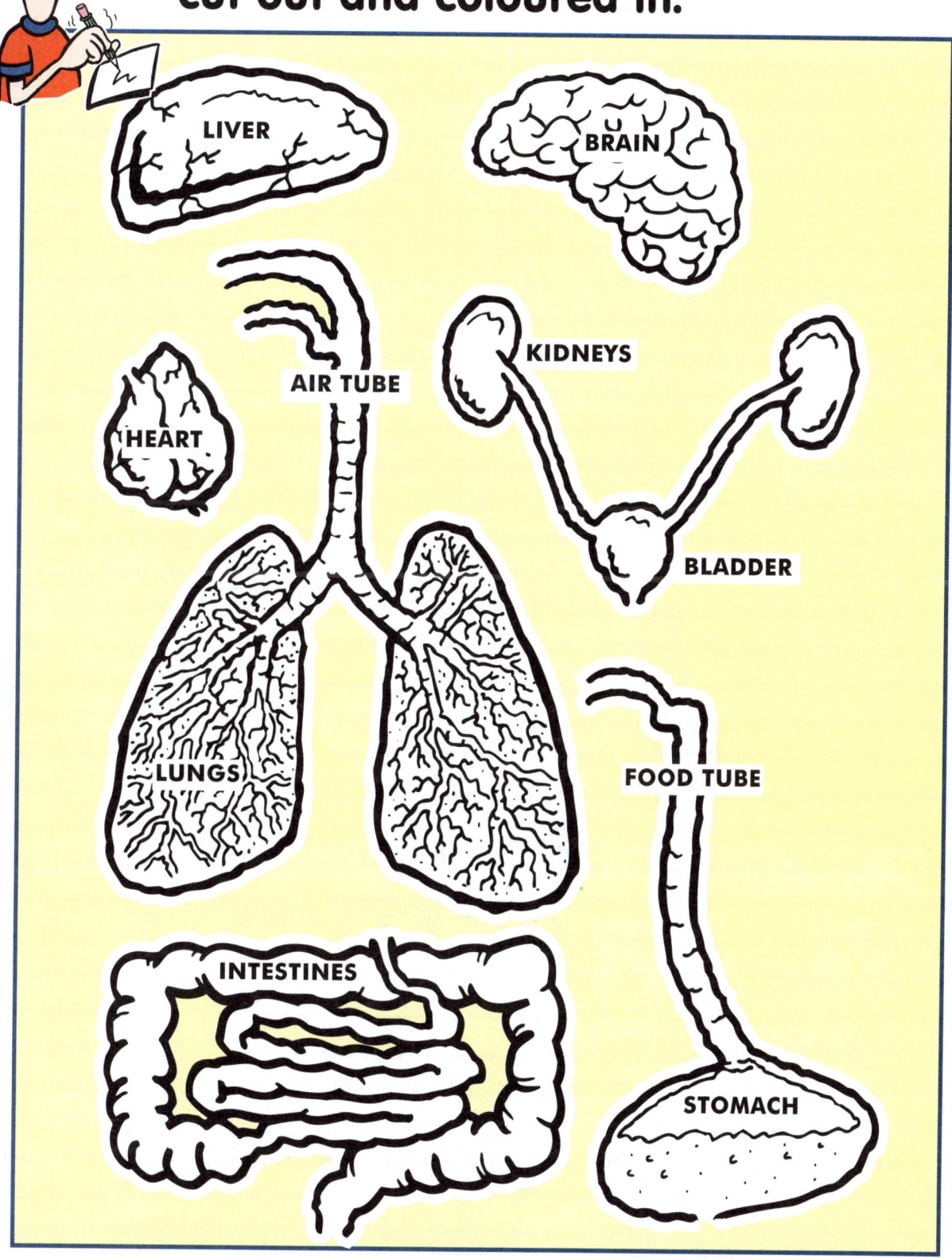

LIVER

BRAIN

HEART

AIR TUBE

KIDNEYS

BLADDER

LUNGS

FOOD TUBE

INTESTINES

STOMACH

My Body 47

5 My Body

Inside Knowledge

Now you can see what the inside of your body looks like. **Have you decided what each organ does?** Try answering these questions - the answers are all organs that you have just coloured in.

1. When your .... squeezes, it pumps blood round your body.

2. When you breathe in, your .... fill up with air. People who smoke may cause harm to this organ.

3. This organ is your body's control centre. Your .... sends messages to and receives them from other organs in your body.

4. When you take a deep breath, your .... takes oxygen to your lungs.

5. Your .... can be as long as 8m. When you eat food it is passed through this organ and all the goodness is taken out. All waste is taken away and leaves your body when you go to the toilet.

6. Your .... links your mouth to the inside of your body. When you eat or drink, the food or liquid passes down this tube to your stomach.

7. In the .... food is churned up, broken down and digested.

8. Your .... are a pair of very hard working filters that purify your blood by taking waste products from it. They also control how much water there is in your body.

9. One of the most important jobs of your .... is to store digested food. It also helps your body get rid of harmful poisons.

10. Waste water and chemicals are turned into urine and stored in your ....

5 My Body

Breathing

All our body cells need oxygen which the body gathers every time you breathe in air through your nose or mouth. The air goes into your lungs and just like moving muscles, you don't have to think about it, your brain does it all for you!

When you breathe in, do it through your nose not your mouth. Inside your nose are lots of tiny hairs that help to filter and take out dust. They also help to warm up the air.

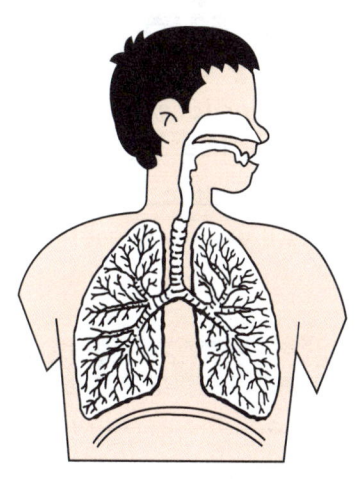

The air goes down a pipe called your trachea which then branches into two, and takes the air into your lungs. Your lungs are like sponges. As the air enters, little air sacs, which are smaller than a pinhead, expand. On the outside of the air sacs are very tiny tubes called capillaries, which take the oxygen out of the air and pass it into the bloodstream.

When you breathe out, the capillaries are also important. They help get rid of another gas called carbon dioxide which your body doesn't need. The capillaries push this gas into the air sacs and we breathe it out.

The lungs are controlled by a muscle that is called the diaphragm. As with all muscles, it is controlled by the brain. When the diaphragm goes up, it pushes air out. When it goes down, air rushes in.

Put your hand on your chest now and take a deep breath. Now let it out. Can you feel how the diaphragm is working?

1. Why should you breathe through your nose?
   _____

2. Which pipe does the air go down?
   _____

3. Why are capillaries important when you breathe out?
   _____

4. What is the diaphragm and what does it do?
   _____

REMEMBER THAT SMOKING CAN DAMAGE YOUR LUNGS – YOUR LUNGS NEED OXYGEN NOT DIRTY, POISONOUS SMOKE.

6 Taking Control & Bullying

BEWARE

Saying "NO!"...

Will Power faces the same problems as all of us. He finds himself in situations that he does not like. He tries to take control and not be bullied into doing something he doesn't want to. This isn't always easy, but he has learnt different ways to say 'NO!'. He thinks it would be useful if you knew how to say 'NO!'...

SAY 'NO' AND MEAN 'NO'...
- Look the person in the eye.
- Stand up straight with your head up.
- Say 'NO' firmly.

BE A BROKEN RECORD...
- If you don't want to do something, keep saying so.
- Stick to one reply.

NO, I DON'T WANT TO.
NO THANK YOU.
NO, I REALLY DON'T WANT TO.

USE FOGGING...
- Don't get into an argument.
- Don't rise to the bait.

SO YOU SAY.
YOU MIGHT SAY SO.

AVOID THE SITUATION...
- If you know places where there could be trouble - avoid them.
- Take another route.
- Walk away immediately if you come across a nasty situation.

COLD SHOULDER...
- Just ignore the person.
- Don't look at them.
- Walk away.

POSITIVE SELF TALK...
- Talk to yourself inside your head.
- Tell yourself you're great.
- Think about all the things you're good at.

I AM OK. I LIKE ME.

Taking Control & Bullying

6 Taking Control & Bullying

BEWARE

What would you do?

Look at the situations below, decide which way of saying 'NO' would be best. There may be more than one way that could work. Write down which you think would work.

☐ You are walking through the park. You see some children from your school smoking...

☐ A friend of yours offers you a cigarette...

☐ A group of children are calling you names. You need to walk past to get home... *"GO AWAY. HA HA"*

☐ A bully at school is asking for your crisps. You want them... *"GIVE US YOUR CRISPS!"*

Could you act out these situations?

Taking Control & Bullying — 51

6 Taking Control & Bullying

Be Aware...

Have you ever found yourself in a difficult situation?
What did you do?
How did it make you feel?

CONSIDER...
Have you ever been offered cigarettes or alcohol?

_____
_____
_____
_____

What did you say?

_____
_____
_____
_____
_____
_____

Why?

_____
_____
_____
_____
_____
_____

There are many things which can influence what you say. You may need to ask yourself some questions before you reply, similar to those on the following page.

52   Taking Control & Bullying

6 Taking Control & Bullying

BEWARE

WHAT IS IT?

HOW WILL IT AFFECT ME?

WILL IT MAKE ME SICK?

DO I KNOW THE PERSON WHO IS OFFERING IT TO ME?

WHAT WILL OTHER PEOPLE THINK OF ME?

WHAT HAPPENS IF I REFUSE?

WHY ARE THEY OFFERING IT TO ME?

WHAT WILL MUM AND DAD SAY IF THEY FIND OUT?

6 Taking Control & Bullying

BEWARE

How do I feel about myself?

Sometimes it is difficult to recognise your own good points.

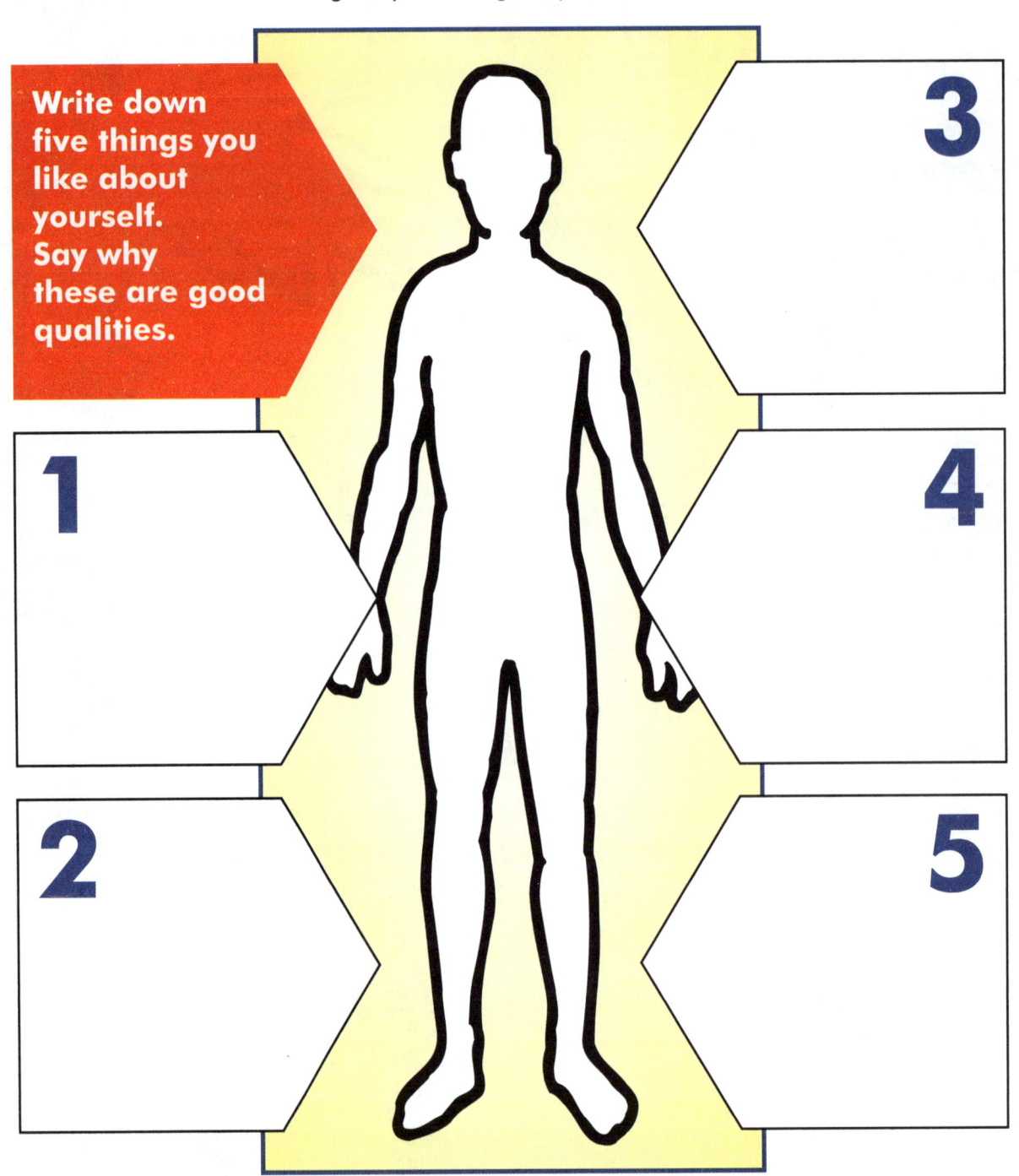

Write down five things you like about yourself. Say why these are good qualities.

1

2

3

4

5

How easy did you find that to do? People are brought up not to be boastful or big headed and sometimes we feel uneasy about saying we are good at something. We play down some qualities and build up others like passing exams.

54   Taking Control & Bullying

6 Taking Control & Bullying

How do I feel about myself?

We usually choose friends because of their good qualities, sometimes other people might not notice these qualities or just ignore them. People who are helpful or thoughtful might not be noticed as much as someone who is funny.

**Can you think of any qualities that get ignored?
Can you say why they are good qualities?**

_____
_____
_____
_____
_____
_____
_____

What qualities do you think are over-rated? Why are they over-rated?

_____
_____
_____
_____
_____
_____

Can you think of any situations where you felt better about yourself because of the way in which someone treated you? How many examples can you think of?

_____
_____
_____
_____
_____
_____
_____

6 Taking Control & Bullying

Advertising

Advertising can have a very strong influence on what decisions we make, especially when it comes to buying particular products.

Here are three examples of places where you can find adverts?

Can you think of four more examples?

1

2

3

4

Adverts can be very clever. They don't just show a picture of the product and tell you why it is the best available, they often have a hidden message too. It is often this part of the advert that you remember without actually realising it buntil you next go to the shops.

6 Taking Control & Bullying

BEWARE

With some classmates, look through some old magazines and newspapers. Fill in the following checklist for each advert you choose:

1. **What is the advert for?**
   _____
   _____

2. **Do you like the advert?**
   Why?
   _____
   _____
   _____

3. **Who do you think it is aimed at?**
   ☐ Men?   ☐ Women?   ☐ Children?   ☐ Everyone?

4. **Is there anything the advert doesn't tell you, that you want to know?**
   _____
   _____

5. **Can you think of the names of other products that may be advertised this way?**
   _____
   _____
   _____
   _____

Do you have a favourite advert? What is it?
_____

What do you like about it?
_____
_____
_____

Taking Control & Bullying   57

6 Taking Control & Bullying

BEWARE

Selling Concepts to Customers

As well as words and pictures, adverts use special techniques to help sell products. Listed below are some of these techniques.

- ☐ Comparison
- ☐ Humour
- ☐ Value for money
- ☐ Using famous people
- ☐ Using groups of people
- ☐ Attention grabbing shock tactics
- ☐ Fun
- ☐ Sex appeal
- ☐ Snob value

Next time you see an advert, think about what techniques they are using.
Do you still want to buy their product?

58   Taking Control & Bullying

6 Taking Control & Bullying

BEWARE

Promotions

Now you know the techniques, can you write down which one is used to help sell the following products. Think about the product and who it is aimed at. Some products may use more than one technique.

Washing Powder	Bottle of Beer	Cigarettes	Motor Car
Chocolates	Breakfast Cereals	Banks	Holidays
Crisps	Supermarkets	Dog Food	Kitchen Cleaner

Taking Control & Bullying 59

6 Taking Control & Bullying

BEWARE

Back to adverts again...

Now it's time to produce an advert of your own.

You have just finished developing a brand new non-alcoholic drink. You want to place a colour advert in the local newspaper.

Before you draw your advert you must think about the following things:

- What is it called – it needs a catchy title!
- Who is it aimed at?
- What technique, or techniques are you going to use?
- What image are you going to use to advertise your product?
- Think about the attractiveness of the overall design.
- Don't use too many words because people won't bother to read them all.
- Are you going to include the price?
- Remember the advert is in colour – what colours are you going to use?

6 Taking Control & Bullying

Advertising Exercise

Name of Product: _____

Aimed at: _____

6 Taking Control & Bullying

BEWARE

Class Activities

Discuss the following with your teacher and classmates.

What do you think about the anti-smoking laws that have been introduced in the USA? Do you think similar regulations will be introduced here in public places, restaurants and pubs?
_____

Why do companies that make alcohol and tobacco sponsor sporting events like snooker and horse racing?
_____

Why do you think Alcopop type drinks are popular and which age group do you think they are aimed at?
_____

Do people at your school encourage others to do things that they don't want to do? Are these people real friends?
_____

Ask your head teacher if you could carry out a School Survey on Bullying

You could ask:

Have you been bullied?   Yes ☐ No ☐   Are you being bullied now?   Yes ☐ No ☐
Did you tell anyone?   Yes ☐ No ☐   Did the bullying stop?   Yes ☐ No ☐
If not, why? _____
Where did the bullying happen? _____
What would you like to see happen next? _____

Collect the information in a graph to show the number of people who have been bullied in each year group. Is the problem evenly spread amongst boys and girls?

7 Answers

True or False (Page 6)   All the statements are true.

Smoking Quiz (Page 9)

1. Lungs   2. Nicotine   3. Tar   4. Breath   5. Passive   6. Health   7. Tobacco   8. Oxygen.

Alcoholic and Non-Alcoholic (Page 18)

<u>Alcoholic</u>: Whisky, alcopop, wine, lager, bitter. <u>Non-Alcoholic</u>: Coke, lemonade, orange juice.

Alcoholic & Non-Alcoholic (Page 27)

| 1. Lager | 2. Lime | 3. Wine | 4. Cider | 5. Whisky | 6. Milk |
| 7. Brandy | 8. Tea | 9. Gin | 10. Cola | 11. Beer | 12. Champagne |

Wordsearch (Page 28)

1. LAGER
2. LIME
3. WINE
4. CIDER
5. WHISKY
6. MILK,
7. BRANDY
8. TEA
9. GIN
10. COLA
11. BEER
12. CHAMPAGNE

A VISIT TO A COUNTRY PUB (Page 31)

MUM		GRANDAD		NANA MEL		KAREN		TIM		WILL POWER	
COST	UNITS	COST	UNITS	COST	UNITS	COST	UNITS	COST	UNITS	COST	UNITS
£1.00	0	£1.10	⅓	£4.50	3	£3.45	4½	£3.00	0	£1.00	0
£2.00	0	£0.50	0	£2.00	0	£0.50	0	£1.00	0	£1.00	0
£0.50	0	£1.00	0							£0.50	0
£3.50	0	£2.60	⅓	£6.50	3	£3.95	4½	£4.00	0	£2.50	0

A visit to a country pub (Page 32)

1. £23.05, 2. Karen, 3. They are too young to drink alcohol,
4. Mum as she drank no alcohol, she knows it's right not to drink and drive, 5. £276.60.

What are Drugs (Page 35)

<u>Tobacco</u>: Can cause cancer, Leaves tar on your lungs, nicotine makes your heart beat faster.
<u>Alcohol</u>: Can cause liver disease, Kills brain cells, Slows down brain activity.

Inside Knowledge (Page 48)

1. Heart   2. Lungs   3. Brain   4. Air Tube   5. Intestines
6. Food Tube   7. Stomach   8. Kidneys   9. Liver   10. Bladder

Answers/Contacts 63

7 Contacts

Smoking

ASH (Action on Smoking and Health)
102-108 Clifton Street, London EC2A 4HW
Tel: 020 7739 5902
Website: http://www.ash.org.uk

ASH Northern Ireland - Ulster Cancer Foundation, 40-42 Eglantine Avenue, Belfast BT9 6DX
Tel: 028 9066 3281

ASH Scotland - 8 Frederick Street, Edinburgh EH2 2HB. Tel: 0131 225 4725

ASH Wales - 374 Cowbridge Road East, Canton, Cardiff CF5 1GY. Tel: 029 2064 1101

QUIT - Ground Floor, 211 Old Street, London EC1V 9NR. Tel: 020 7251 1551
Tel: 01232 663439 (Northern Ireland)
Website: http://www.quit.org.uk

QUITLINE - Tel: 0800 00 22 00 (freephone)

Drugs

ADFAM - Tel: 0207 928 8900

DRUGSCOPE
32-36 Loman Street, London SE1 0EE
Tel: 020 7928 1211
Website: http://www.drugscope.org.uk

DRUG ACTION TEAM
Search for your local team on the internet

HEALTH EDUCATION AUTHORITY
Trevelyan House, 30 Great Peter Street, London SW1P 2HW. Tel: 0207 222 5300
Website: http://www.hea.org.uk

NATIONAL DRUGS HELPLINE
Tel: 0800 77 66 00 (freephone 24-hour)

RELEASE - Tel: 0207 603 8654 (24-hour)
Website: http://www.release.org.uk

RE-SOLV - Tel: 0808 800 2345 (freephone)
Website: www.re-solv.org

RELEASE DRUGS IN SCHOOLS ADVICE
Tel: 08457 36 66 66 (Mon-Fri 10am-5pm)

SOLVENT ABUSE RESOURCE GROUP
28 Penny Street, Blackburn BB1 6HL
Tel: 01254 677493
Website: http://www.airtime.co.uk

TACADE - 1 Hulme Place, The Crescent, Salford, Greater Manchester M5 4QA
Tel: 0161 745 8925

Alcohol

AL-ANON FAMILY GROUPS UK & EIRE
61 Great Dover Street, London, SE1 4YF
Tel: 020 7403 0888 (24-hour)
Website: http://www.al-anonuk.org.uk

ALCOHOLICS ANONYMOUS
PO Box 1, Stonebow House, Stonebow, York YO1 7NJ. Tel: 01904 644026
Website: http://www.alcohol-anonymous.org.uk

ALCOHOL CONCERN
Waterbridge House, 32-36 Loman Street, London SE1 0EE. Tel: 020 7928 7377
Website: http://www.alcoholconcern.org.uk

NACOA The National Association for Children of Alcoholics
PO Box 64, Fishponds, Bristol BS16 2UH
Website: http://www.nacoa.org.uk

DRINKLINE - Tel: 0800 917 8282 (freephone)

SCOTTISH COUNCIL ON ALCOHOL
137-145 Sauchiehall Street, Glasgow G3 3EW
Tel: 0141 333 9677

WRECKED - Website: http://www.wrecked.co.uk

Other Useful Contacts

CHILDLINE - Tel: 0800 1111 (freephone)
Website: http://www.childline.org.uk

COMMISSION FOR RACIAL EQUALITY - 0207 828 7022
Website: http://www.cre.gov.uk

CRIMESTOPPERS - 0800 555 111

HEALTH PROMOTION WALES
Ffynnon-las, Ty Glas Avenue, Llanishen, Cardiff CF14 5EZ. Tel: 01222 752222
Website: http://www.hpw.org.uk

HEBS Health education for scotland
Woodburn House, Canaan Lane, Edinburgh EH10 4SG. Tel: 0131 536 5500
Website: http://www.hebs.scot.nhs.uk

NSPCC HELPLINE - 0800 800 500
Website: http://www.nspcc.org.uk or www.there4me.com

THE SAMARITANS - 08457 90 90 90
Website: http://www.samaritans.org.uk

VICTIM SUPPORT - 0207 735 9166
Website: http://www.victim support.org.uk